*Rebirth of Wonder:
Epiphanies at Winter Solstice*

Rebirth of Wonder:

Epiphanies at Winter Solstice

CAROLYN KELLEY WILLIAMS

Copyright © 2022 by Carolyn Kelley Williams.

All rights reserved. No part of this book may be reproduced or used in any manner without written permission of the copyright owner except for the use of quotations in a book review.

First paperback edition February 2022.

Stonehenge photograph by Andy Powell (2009), generously made available through a Creative Commons Attribution 2.0 Generic License.

For Fred, my Rapture

Table of Contents

Foreword	ix
Out of Dark Times	3
Pilgrim	4
In This Cup of Mountains	6
All This Loss	7
Truths	8
Lessons	9
For This We Have Come	10
The Turning	12
Rebirth of Wonder	13
Glastonbury Cathedral	14
We Dream a Golden Child	15
The Birth	16
The Coming	17
Eternal Return	18
About the Author	21

Foreword

The great cycle of seasons has no beginning and no end. It flows around and through us ceaselessly, whether or not we realize how it forms our physical life and informs our spirit. We each step into its flow at our own moment and our life is moved according to its impulses and urgings. Our psyche also resonates with the cycle of seasons and is moved by the journey of the earth through its cosmic patterns. This is perhaps especially noticeable at the winter solstice, when the earth is farthest from the sun and our planet seems to pause in utter darkness before it begins its journey into light. This potent time of cosmic shift stirs us deeply and has ever symbolized endings and new beginnings.

The darkness at winter solstice, and its related fallow periods, which in the northern hemisphere happen around December 21, fill us with unease. Our psyche shifts, so that everywhere we look, we notice the desolation of decay and endings. From this perspective, things seem to lose their power and significance, their meaning.

We humans cannot long endure life without meaning. In dark and desolate times, persons in many cultures have gone on pilgrimage, yearning to find renewal at the center—the sacred source from which transcendent radiance pours into the field of time. Our ancestors, seeking to evoke and experience the sacred, carved magical symbols on the walls of caves or erected massive standing stones in alignment with the heavens. They built cities and temples patterned on the stars, danced solemn and stylized dances, knelt at archaic altars to whisper prayers. Today, we may not respond in exactly these ways, but even in our secular culture, dark times bereft of meaning call for symbols, the power of ritual, and pilgrimage.

Making a pilgrimage means leaving ordinary time to begin a journey of renewal, seeking new creativity and vision, new stirrings of passion for our existence, a new capacity to love whatever it is we love, and new courage to do what most matters for us to do. The journey may take the pilgrim to places long known to be sacred—Stonehenge, Bethlehem, Benares. Or it may lead to ordinary, humble places—like the lagoons and paths of a city park, or a wayside chapel at a country crossroads. Wherever our pilgrimage takes us, we enter a path of heightened awareness. Often, we know neither what we are seeking, nor how we will recognize it if we find it.

Like all pilgrims, the pilgrims in the poems contained here have been moved by inner urgings that defy logic. There is never a guarantee of epiphany or a promise that we will find renewal. Pilgrimage has always been an act of faith, or desperation. Often, it's a long ordeal, with wrong turns, faltering, deprivation, and discouragement before we can say, "For this we have come."

Like the Ancients whose deep dreams we dream, whose memories we almost remember, who stir in our cells and haunt the depths of our being, at winter solstice we yearn for light from darkness more than physical darkness, for birth more than physical birth. There comes a dawning in the womb-cave of the self with its symbol-laden ancestral depths. Radiance arises. A subtle stirring at first becomes a pulsing flow of new life-energy. Something marvelous within us awakens and begins its inexorable journey into light, moving toward fullest expression in the season of blossoming and fruition of what will be, but is not yet.

Poems

Out of Dark Times

On our arduous journey through this darkening world
with its waning energies, outmoded forms, all that must be forsaken,
the savaging of innocence, rogue madmen crushing cultures,
whole species lost, and temples and treasured forests reduced to ashes—
we, weary, often blinded by tears,
yearn for renewal.

In such times, Ancients, going to earth,
stood reverent and awed in temple-caves,
attending, at certain moments, the passing of light through
deep mysterious chambers carved with symbols that gradually
grew bright.

Is there still a turning point, as the Ancients believed,
when radiance is born of boundless void?
When something comes from nothing?
Are miracles still possible—even now, even for us?

Listen.
A pulse in deepest darkness.
Harmonies ring in our bones.

See.
Light, holy and golden, comes.

Pilgrim

Pilgrim! Blessings on this longest night of the year,
this darkest time. Shall we share a path, be Magi together?
Even in the shadow of your cloak, your yearning eyes shine out,
intense—you have the look of one set loose from common things,
someone now faithful to an inner call.

Silence awhile, the only sound our footsteps.

May I speak again? In another time, an indescribable blaze
would have drawn us on, would it not?
Yet now, it is not up there among the stars,
lovely though they are.
It's here within us, and difficult, often, to trust.
Did I hear you sigh?

One cannot calculate how long such journeying has drawn us on.

Endless this path. Arduous. How weary I am.
Yet you seem tireless, dear pilgrim, while I am filled with sorrow
and emptied out from all those endings.
Alone I might not have soldiered on.
Thank you for your company.

Another timeless time.

Doubts congeal in shadows. We suffer burning thirst.
Then, when darkness is most profound, a gleam!

A radiance! And—how shall I say it? Unfathomable peace.
Look, my pilgrim! Do you see it?
Have we arrived? Is our pilgrimage fulfilled?
Shall we fall to our knees?
Be redeemed?
Made whole?

Ah . . .

In This Cup of Mountains

Amid sun-splash and dazzle,
winter is subtle.

Occasional leaves turn brittle, wither,
are blown across stony sand.

The ocotillo's narrow shadows
slide up adobe walls.

Stones are sepia, purple, rust,
and enormous, placed not by Ancients
to mark the solstice dawning
but raised by the earth itself,
out of itself.

Whatever the landscape,
there comes a turning within
to a certain darkness
we know as human, personal.
We suffer it, sing of it, weep,
the darkness is so intense.

Then—this is told and retold—light.
Light we yearn for returns
so marvelous we can scarcely speak of it.
Yet we do: We call it *holy*.

All This Loss

This dying everywhere.
The country beasts—neglected, mute,
shuddering in frozen mud.
Our beautiful young—despairing.
Teachings, once wise, turned cruel.
Libraries burned.
Even our gentle gardens, weeds.

Was this not prophesied?
Is this not wasteland?
Is this the end of days?

In the darkness we search our hearts for comfort.
Turning within, we struggle to remember—what?
We've been here before.
There were standing stones, then,
that were swept with radiance.
And after all our doubt, our waiting,
the sun returned.

And, yes, there was a point of light some called a star,
drawing us—if we followed—toward transformation.
Roots grew hot with eros,
and branches budded with promise.
Our midnights were not midnight forever,
and lambs were born, and frozen rivers
began again to flow.

Truths

Just as the Ancients
when their disordered world wound down
wandered the desert, lonely and afraid,
ate thistles and sand, were fed by ravens—
as the Ancients did, we call such disorder wasteland,
suffer a darkness that brings no rest, no rich renewal,
holds only despair.

But what the Ancients knew we now remember:
The solstice sun returns, blessing the stones.
David, the Sacred King, dances us into the temple.
Green Man ever utters forth his leaves.
The Chalice refreshes our thirsting souls.
And the Star, blazing across the heavens,
guides us to the Child of Wonder.

Lessons

Teach us, winter fields,
the wisdom of deep dreaming.

Teach us, seeds,
to love the necessary dark,
trusting that turning time
will ever bring forth green.

Bright, ribboned gifts,
teach us abundance.
Christmas morning children,
teach us hope.

Traditions, teach us how our beloved dead
still gather, unseen, to bless us
as we light the candles,
speak the ancient words,
lift ornaments to trees.

Wise Ones of the East, teach us
how truth comes not by expectation.
Show us, with your star,
that humble, holy place
where life begins anew,
and right, and beautiful,
that we may kneel in reverence,
offer frankincense and myrrh.

For This We Have Come

Something in sorrowful darkness
stirs us awake. Scarcely knowing why,
we prepare for a journey,
stir ashes for portents,
study the stars.

Reason watches, skeptical,
assuring us that pilgrimage is foolish.
We'll squander comfort, certainty,
all we thought we knew.

Then something uncanny—
something someone in another time
might have called a star,
but not such a star
as anyone has ever seen—
draws us out and away.
We go.

This star, if you could call it that,
does not blaze across heaven
showing us our course.
We are no Wise Men.
Many times, we falter,
consider turning back.
At last, bone-tired,
weary unto death,
we stop.

Suddenly, at the center of darkness,
something powerful, yet peaceful,
shines—something we know is true.
For this we have come.

The Turning

Yes. These times are dark—
the familiar darkness of winter solstice.
But also the terrible darkness
of humankind.

We study history. We learn
the Ancients, too, knew darkness.
Ancients! Where did you find endurance,
hope? How did you come to grace?

Go to the stones, they whisper,
those long-since tumbled temples
we patterned on the stars,
the ever-transforming moon,
the nightly-disappearing sun,
all dancing their dances perfectly.

Their lesson is this: The sun,
at the darkest moment of the turning year,
returns to touch the scattered stones, the weeds,
our upturned faces, our sorrowing hearts
with radiance. The light returns.
But darkness always comes again.
That is the cosmic plan.
That, too, the dreadful pattern of humankind.
But then, when darkness seems unbearable,
again, and ever again, a blessed radiance.

Rebirth of Wonder

Never has darkness seemed so dense,
our offerings such ashes in our hands.
Ancient patterns are fragmented,
once-lovely containers shards that cut our fingers.
The center is forgotten, perhaps is no longer even there.

Still, weary, too foolish to despair,
we heave ourselves from beds
because we always have,
and come here once again,
our hair disheveled.
You would not recognize us
for what we are—celebrants, pilgrims,
the faintest shadows of our uncles
with their camels, their frankincense, their star.

But still, we've come
to this seemingly ordinary place
to know rebirth of wonder, to know
light pouring once again into our world,
and order.

Back home again, we cannot agree on what occurred—
only that where there was darkness
and weariness and disarray,
there now is light, renewal, peace.
We see anew the beauty of those we love.
Our simple acts seem, somehow, holy,
our hearts more open.

Glastonbury Cathedral

A cathedral once stood, magnificent,
where now the winter grass is gray,
like the sky, like the mute, stark ruin
bereft of its buttresses and vaulted ceilings,
its echoes of chanting voices and whispered prayers.
Not a single fragment of chalice, trumpeting angel, saint,
or Virgin's cobalt robe resplendent and glorious remains.

We wait in the chill, the only sound the wind.
Soon, on this longest night, darkness will prevail.
We turn inward to darkness within ourselves;
fear stirs—we're so in love with light.

Yet we await the mystery. Like bread being kneaded,
pressed, and pressed again, we are pulled apart,
and turned and shaped. Whatever we were
is transformed into what we will become.

And then we're awake, our cheeks and eyelids golden.
The sun returns. And look! The hawthorn,
which yesterday was bleak and empty of leaves,
is white with blossoms.

We Dream a Golden Child

Soon will be the longest night,
the sun, in its turning, farthest
from our blessed earth, our blessed lives.
We know in our bones
a terrible dread.

Like our ancestors huddled in darkness,
we shudder. Some of us pray.
Some study the heavens.
Some counter darkness with divinations
and revels, reckless dancing,
laughter edged with fear.

Sleep brings strange dreams.
We seem to see a wonderful birth
in a humble, unexpected place.
Mysterious voices whisper
names we cannot comprehend.

Then morning. Sunlight dazzles.
Out of utter darkness, light returns.
The sun is born again.
As the Ancients have done since the beginning,
we celebrate a sacred,
deeply sustaining feast
and are filled with grace.

The Birth

All night long we huddle together,
shivering. A woman, nearing her time,
turns and turns in the dark.
Everything is pain.
There are animals here,
and simple people.
Her husband worries close by.
Someone has softened her place with straw.
Waiting is long, and difficult.

Then, a sliver of light,
becoming a luminous crown.
Radiance spreads over the straw,
over our wondering faces.
We are bathed in light.

The child comes forth.
We forget our common concerns
and, in the golden light, rejoice.

The Coming

Who among us will welcome this child?
We notice thunder on the horizon,
an extraordinary blaze of stars,
alignment of planets.
And yet, we are afraid.

Who among us will welcome this child?
Its destiny in a harsh and unjust world
breaks our hearts, stirs an almost unbearable love,
moves us to tears.

Who among us will welcome this child?
The coming changes all we know,
and somewhere, forces mobilize,
begin their terrible march,
determined that it must not be.

Who among us will welcome this child?
It dazzles us with its glory,
and stirs such awe, we are stunned,
overcome with rapture,
transformed.

Eternal Return

Darkness again, alas,
more dreadful than before,
and humankind more enthralled by lies.
Where does a hand offer kindness,
a heart compassion, an intellect justice,
a spirit truth? Despairing, we grapple
with ugliness in history,
and in ourselves.

And doing this,
we discover the dance of atoms,
hear music in choruses of trees,
treasure the tiniest insects,
honor, even, death.
Seeing our fragile planet from afar
we are moved to cherishing.

Yet this solstice darkness mirrors a dark and dreadful
human time. What meaning shall we give it?
What have we learned from our pilgrimages,
from all that searching?

We see that solstice darkness surrenders to light,
and human darkness is transformed, though slowly.
Grief is inescapable, yet life returns,
the eternal return we call rebirth.
Gratitude now fills our hearts. And hope.

This we know:
Each time the radiance returns,
spirit utters forth its magnitude.
Light pours again into our lives
like a solstice sunrise.

About the Author

Carolyn Kelley Williams, a founding member of the performance ensemble *World Enough & Time*, has appeared with poet Zoe Keithley and flutist Kathy Kelley-Hahn in Midwestern theatres, churches, and cabarets. A leader for the *Intensive Journal*® program created by Dr. Ira Progoff, she presents writing workshops throughout the US—and, since 2019, on Zoom. For more than thirty years, she was managing editor of several international scientific publications. In 1991, she participated in a writing workshop taught by Mary Oliver at Bennington College. Her collection, *Inexhaustible Offering: Lincoln Park Poems*, is available on Amazon. She lives in Phoenix, where she writes, teaches, and creates stained glass art.

Acknowledgment

Thanks to Andrew Durkin, of Yellow Bike Press, whose brilliant editorial skills and artistic sensibilities, because he is himself an artist, have made *Rebirth of Wonder* a true collaboration.